WITHDRAWN

RELIGIONS AROUND THE WORLD

Protestantism

Katy Gerner

Marshall Cavendish
Benchmark
New York

This edition first published in 2009 in the United States of America by Marshall Cavendish Benchmark.

Marshall Cavendish Benchmark
99 White Plains Road
Tarrytown, NY 10591
www.marshallcavendish.us

First published in 2008 by
MACMILLAN EDUCATION AUSTRALIA PTY LTD
15–19 Claremont Street, South Yarra 3141

Visit our website at www.macmillan.com.au or go directly to www.macmillanlibrary.com.au

Associated companies and representatives throughout the world.

Copyright © Katy Gerner 2008

Library of Congress Cataloging-in-Publication Data

Gerner, Katy.
    Protestantism / by Katy Gerner.
        p. cm. — (Religions around the world)
    Includes index.
    ISBN 978-0-7614-3173-2
    1. Protestantism. I. Title.
    BX4811.3.G47 2008
280'.4—dc22

                                2008002856

Edited by Erin Richards
Text and cover design by Cristina Neri, Canary Graphic Design
Photo research by Legend Images
Illustrations on pp. 6 and 14 by Andy Craig and Nives Porcellato
Map courtesy of Geo Atlas; modified by Raul Diche

Printed in the United States

Acknowledgments

The author would like to thank Patricia Hayward for her suggestions, her wisdom and her time spent reviewing this book.

The author and the publisher are grateful to the following for permission to reproduce copyright material:

Front cover photograph (main): Young man being baptised in Sea of Galilee, Israel © Rosebud Pictures/Stone+/Getty Images. Other images: Bible © christine balderas/iStockphoto; church © Stuart Monk/iStockphoto; church steeple © Sondra Paulson/iStockphoto; wooden cross © Gillian Mowbray/iStockphoto; Lutheran Rose courtesy of The Lutheran Church–Missouri Synod; book background © Felix Möckel/ iStockphoto.

Photos courtesy of: AAP Image/AFP PHOTO, 24 (top); © Ted Spiegel/CORBIS, 21 (top left); Getty Images, 13 (top center); The English School/The Bridgeman Art Library/Getty Images, 18; Chad Buchanan/Getty Images, 20 (bottom); Digital Vision/Getty Images, 6 (bottom), 7; Hulton Archive/Getty Images, 18 (bottom left); Photo by Richard Koek/Getty Images, 20 (top); Peter Macdiarmid/Getty Images, 25 (top); Prestige/Newsmakers/Getty Images, 28 (bottom); Photodisc/Getty Images, 23 (bottom right); David Silverman/Getty Images, 17 (center); Stockbyte/Getty Images, 22 ; Maury Phillips/WireImage/Getty Images, 9 (bottom right); © christine balderas/iStockphoto, 3 (bottom), 10 (top right); © Aman Khan/iStockphoto, 4 (bottom center left); © Geir-Olav Lyngfjell/iStockphoto, 16 (top); © Vasko Miokovic/ iStockphoto, 4 (center); © Gillian Mowbray/iStockphoto, 1 (center), 31; © Owusu-Ansah/iStockphoto, 4 (bottom center right), 30 (top); © Sondra Paulson/iStockphoto, 3 (top center); © Nina Shannon/iStockphoto, 21 (bottom left); © Richard Stamper/iStockphoto, 4 (bottom right); © Bob Thomas/iStockphoto, 4 (bottom left); NASA Goddard Space Flight Center, 4 (center behind); Photos.com, 29 (bottom); The Salvation Army Heritage Center, Sydney, 8 (bottom left), 19 (right); © Peter Baxter/Shutterstock, 17 (bottom left); © Katrina Brown/ Shutterstock, 5 (bottom); © Joe Gough/Shutterstock, 27 (bottom); © Berto Paeli/Shutterstock, 12 (left); © Larry St. Pierre/Shutterstock, 26 (top); © Jozef Sedmak/Shutterstock, 15 (top); © Gordon Swanson/Shutterstock, 4 (top); © Robert Young/Shutterstock, 11.

Photos used in book design: book background © Felix Möckel/iStockphoto, 6, 9, 10, 16, 18, 21; church © Stuart Monk/iStockphoto, 1, 3, 8–9, 10, 23, 25, 27, 30; church steeple © Sondra Paulson/iStockphoto, 3, 5, 8, 13, 14, 16, 18, 21, 24, 28, 32; cross based on image by Georgios Kollidas/Shutterstock, 3; parchment background © Andrey Zyk/iStockphoto, 12, 13, 18, 19; wooden cross © Nina Shannon/ iStockphoto, 13; wooden cross © Gillian Mowbray/iStockphoto, 17.

For Glenn, Warren, and Michael

1 3 5 6 4 2

Contents

World Religions 4

Protestantism 5

Religious Beliefs 6

Beliefs About Behavior 8

Scriptures 10

Religious Leaders 12

Worship Practices 14

Festivals and Celebrations 16

Important Protestants 18

Clothes and Food 20

Birth 22

Growing Up 24

Marriage 26

Death and the Afterlife 28

Protestantism Around the World 30

Glossary 31

Index 32

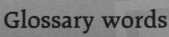

Glossary words

When a word is printed in **bold**, you can look up its meaning in the Glossary on page 31.

World Religions

Religion is a belief in a supernatural power that must be loved, worshipped, and obeyed. A world religion is a religion that is practiced throughout the world. The five core world religions are Christianity, Islam, Hinduism, Buddhism and Judaism.

People practicing a religion follow practices that they believe are pleasing to their god or gods. They read sacred **scriptures** and may worship either privately at home or in a place of worship. They often carry out special rituals, such as when a baby is born, a couple gets married, or someone dies. Religious people have beliefs about how they should behave in this life, and also about life after death.

Learning about world religions can help us to understand each other's differences. We learn about the different ways people try to lead good lives and make the world a better place.

World religions are practiced by many people of different cultures.

Protestantism

Protestantism is one of the three main branches of Christianity. The other two are Catholicism and the Orthodox Church. Each **denomination** has slightly different ways of practicing their religion, such as:

✝ the ways they worship

✝ who they allow to be church leaders

✝ what their churches look like

✝ how they solve certain problems.

Protestants, like all Christians, believe in one god, called God, and that Jesus is the son of God. They believe Jesus came to Earth to teach people the right way to live, and that through his death and **resurrection** they can go to heaven.

Protestantism came about in the 1500s. Some Christians were unhappy with some practices of the Catholic Church and wanted to make changes. The word *Protestant* comes from the word *protest*. Protestant denominations include the Lutheran Church, the Anglican Church, and the Religious Society of Friends, or Quakers. There is also the Baptist Church, the Church of Christ, the Methodist Church, the Seventh-day Adventists, the Salvation Army, and much more recently, the Assemblies of God Church.

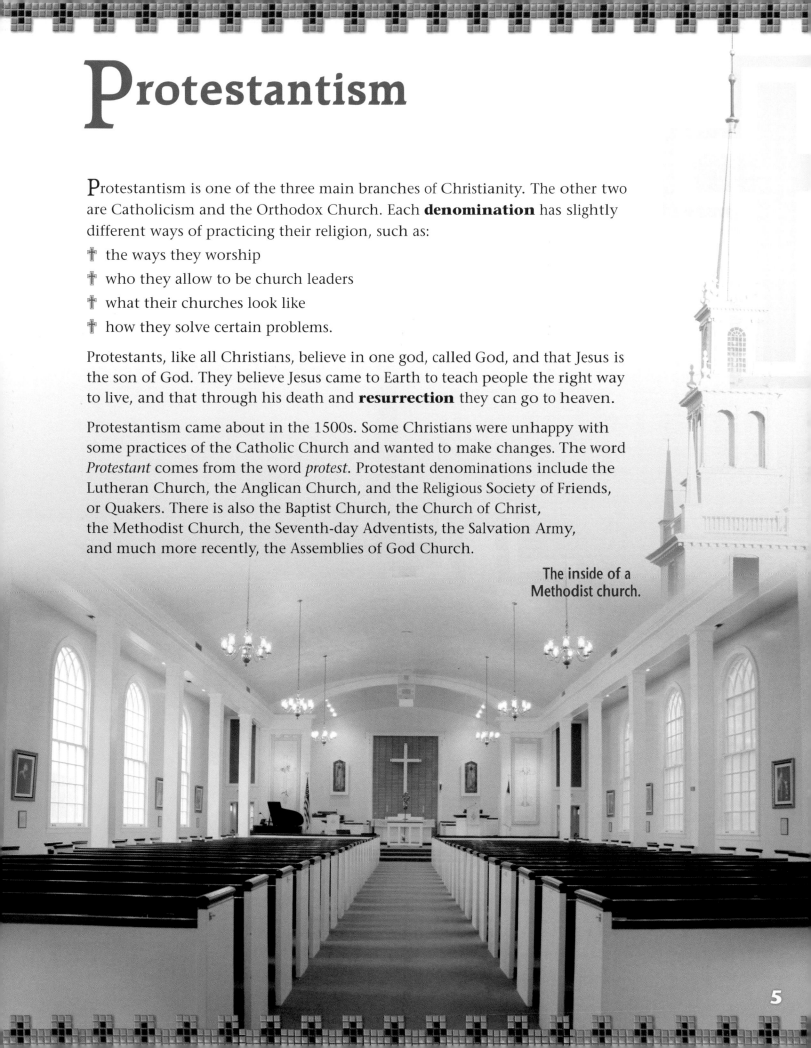

The inside of a Methodist church.

5

Religious Beliefs

Important religious beliefs for Protestants are the belief in the Holy Trinity, the belief that God listens to their prayers, and the belief in serving God in whatever role he chooses for them.

THE LORD'S PRAYER

Our Father in Heaven,
Hallowed be your name,
Your kingdom come,
Your will be done,
On Earth as in Heaven.
Give us today our daily bread.
Forgive us our sins
As we forgive those who sin against us.
Save us from the time of trial
And deliver us from evil.
For the kingdom, the power,
and the glory are yours
Now and for ever. Amen.

The Holy Trinity

Nearly all Protestants believe in the **Holy Trinity**. The Holy Trinity is:

✝ God, the Father, who made Heaven and Earth

✝ Jesus Christ, the son of God, who came to Earth and is the **Messiah**

✝ The Holy Spirit, who guides and strengthens people.

The Holy Trinity is often depicted in a diagram called the Shield of Trinity.

Answered Prayers

Protestants believe they can pray to God and he will answer their prayers. A favorite Protestant prayer is the Lord's Prayer. This was the prayer Jesus taught his **disciples**.

Many Protestant families pray before each meal.

An Anglican priest leads the Holy Communion ceremony in church.

Serving God

Protestants believe that one way to serve God is to become a member of the **clergy**. This leadership position has many names, including priest, minister, and pastor. Clergy are both men and women, although a small number of Protestant churches only allow men to lead church services. In the Protestant Church, clergy can marry and usually live in a house near the church with their family.

Clergy lead church services, conduct weddings and funerals, pray, and preach. Some also run, or work for, Christian organizations, write for Christian newspapers, or teach. Clergy believe God has called them to do the work they do. **Lay people** in the Protestant Church also believe God calls them to spend their life doing his work. Many Protestants do volunteer work.

Beliefs About Behavior

Protestants have a number of beliefs about how they should behave. Protestants believe they should love their neighbor, teach other people about Jesus, and follow Jesus's teachings.

Loving Their Neighbor

Jesus told his **apostles** they should love their neighbor as much as they love themselves. This doesn't just mean being nice to the people next door. It means treating all people the way you would like to be treated, with kindness, love, and respect. There are a large number of Protestant organizations that help people in the community, including the Fellowship of the Least Coin, Baptist World Aid, and the Salvation Army.

Teaching Others About Jesus

Protestants believe that they should preach the good news about what Jesus has done for everyone all over the world. People who go overseas to preach about Jesus are called missionaries. They go to different countries, live in the communities, learn the local language, and then preach about Jesus.

Missionaries often do other things beside preaching about Jesus. They may also provide medical care and food for the community. They teach people to read and write, help to set up small businesses, and teach skills to help people find work.

The Salvation Army provides meals and counseling to firefighters.

Sermon on the Mount

Jesus's most specific teaching about behavior was the Sermon on the Mount. He preached while he was sitting on the side of a mountain near Lake Galilee. He taught the following things:

Archbishop Desmond Tutu campaigned to end apartheid in South Africa.

✝ Love your enemies and forgive them when they do bad things to you

✝ Do not judge other people

✝ Trust and depend on God and do not worry about what you are going to eat, drink, or wear

A famous Protestant who follows these teachings is Archbishop Desmond Tutu of South Africa.

Archbishop Desmond Tutu

Archbishop Desmond Tutu was born in 1931 and became an Anglican priest in 1960. He opposed South Africa's **apartheid** policy, which divided South Africans into racial groups, with white people having all the advantages. His opposition was very brave as many people who protested were imprisoned, had their houses burned down, or were killed. Tutu always preached, and still preaches, the importance of forgiveness. He believes forgiveness stops a person from being filled with hatred and anger. In 1984, Tutu received the Nobel Peace Prize. He became the first black Archbishop of the Anglican Church in South Africa in 1986.

Scriptures

Protestants believe that the Christian Bible is inspired by God. The Bible teaches about God and how Christians should behave. The Protestant Bible is made up of thirty-nine books in the Old Testament and twenty-seven in the New Testament.

The Old Testament

The Old Testament was first written in the ancient Hebrew language. It teaches about law, history, and poetry. It describes why the world was created, how Israel became a nation, and the work done by the kings and the **prophets**. The Old Testament includes the Psalms, which are beautiful poems written to God, and the Proverbs, which give good advice.

The New Testament

The New Testament includes the Gospels, which cover the life and teachings of Jesus. It also includes writings on history and prophecy, and letters to new Christian communities. The letters were mostly written by the apostle Paul.

The Bible is the book of scriptures for Protestants.

O Lord, my heart is not lifted up,
my eyes are not raised too high;
I do not occupy myself with things
too great and too marvelous for me.
But I have calmed and quieted my soul,
like a child quieted at its mother's breast;
like a child that is quieted is my soul.
O Israel, hope in the Lord
from this time forth and for evermore.

PSALM 131
REVISED STANDARD VERSION, 1971

The getting of treasures by a lying tongue is a fleeting vapor and a snare of death.

PROVERBS 21:6
REVISED STANDARD VERSION, 1971

The Gospels

The word *gospel* means *good news* and refers to the good news of what Jesus did for everyone.

The Gospel according to Matthew was written around 70–110 CE. It explains how Jesus fulfilled the Old Testament prophecies of what the Messiah would be like and explains his teachings. The Gospel is believed to have been written for Greek-speaking Jewish Christians and non-Jews familiar with the Hebrew Scriptures.

The Gospel according to Mark was written around 70 CE and was thought to be written for Greek-speaking residents of the Roman Empire. Mark's gospel emphasizes that Jesus was the Messiah and that he suffered. It also explains Jewish customs.

The Gospel according to Luke was written around 60–63 CE, and emphasizes Jesus as the savior of oppressed people. It was written for Christians from a non-Jewish background.

The Gospel according to John was written around 90–120 CE. It explains Christian theology and gives the most information about Jesus' life on Earth.

The Gospels were written by the apostles Matthew, Mark, Luke, and John.

Religious Leaders

MARTIN LUTHER

Two important Protestant religious leaders were Martin Luther and William Tyndale.

Martin Luther 1483–1546 ᴄᴇ

Martin Luther was a Roman Catholic priest and professor in Biblical Studies in Germany. He studied the Bible carefully and felt that the Catholic Church was not being fair. At that time, the Catholic Church taught that people must pay money to the Church to help **souls** leave **purgatory** and go to heaven. As the Bible was only available in Latin, most people could not read it. Luther did not approve of this, and decided to translate the New Testament into German.

Luther also taught that:

✝ sins are forgiven by God, so it is unnecessary to pay the priest to arrange forgiveness for you

✝ you can approach God directly with prayer

✝ the Church is made up of all believers, not just the men at the top

✝ everybody should be able to read the Bible.

By the time Luther died in 1546, a new breakaway church had begun. It was called the Lutheran Church and was based on Luther's teachings. Today, the Lutheran Church is one of the largest Protestant churches, with around 70 million Lutherans worldwide.

Martin Luther believed that the Bible should be available to people in their native language.

William Tyndale's translation of the New Testament was the first ever printed in the English language.

William Tyndale 1494–1536 CE

William Tyndale was a priest, teacher, and scholar who lived in England. He could speak Greek, Latin, Hebrew, Dutch, German, Italian, and Spanish as well as English.

Tyndale translated the New Testament into English from the original Greek and Hebrew texts. He did this even though King Henry VIII ordered him not to. Neither the Catholic Church nor the Church of England approved of him or his translation.

Tyndale believed it was important for everybody to read the Bible for themselves. He had to spend much of his time traveling and hiding so that he was not found until he finished his translation.

Tyndale was eventually caught and burned at the stake. His last words were, "Lord, open the eyes of the King of England." Three years after Tyndale's death, Henry VIII finally published a Bible in English.

Worship Practices

Important worship practices for many Protestants are to attend church services and Bible studies, and to take Holy Communion.

Church Services and Bible Studies

Many Protestants attend church services every Sunday, as well as special services on holy days, such as Christmas Day. At a church service, the clergy member gives a **sermon** and the **congregation** prays and sings hymns together.

Many Protestants also attend Bible studies. Study groups meet in a member's home or in the church hall, usually once a week in the evening. Sometimes study groups are led by clergy, but often they are led by a lay person from the church. At the beginning of each session, there are prayers and a passage read from the Bible. The group then discuss the passage and any related themes. Some groups also play instruments and sing Christian songs. Study groups usually end with tea, coffee, and light snacks.

This is the typical floor plan of a Protestant church.

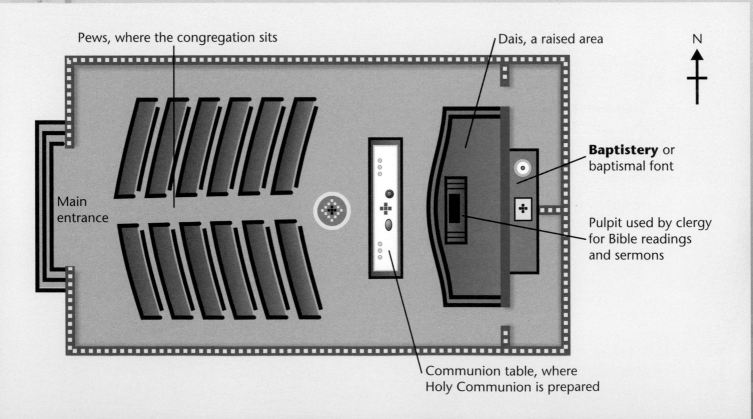

Pews, where the congregation sits

Dais, a raised area

N

Baptistery or baptismal font

Main entrance

Pulpit used by clergy for Bible readings and sermons

Communion table, where Holy Communion is prepared

Jesus shared bread and wine with his disciples during the Last Supper.

Holy Communion

Holy Communion is practiced by nearly all Christian denominations, except the Quakers and the Salvation Army. It is a special time for Christians to remember how much Jesus did for them. It reminds them of the last meal Jesus had with his disciples before he died. This meal is known as the Last Supper.

At Holy Communion, each believer receives a piece of bread and a sip of wine or grape juice.

The people taking Holy Communion consume the bread and wine and pray a thanksgiving prayer.

There are small differences in the way Holy Communion is served in the different denominations. Some churches only allow clergy to officiate at Holy Communion. Others allow lay people to officiate. Some use wine and others use grape juice. Some use ordinary bread and others use wafers or flatbread.

15

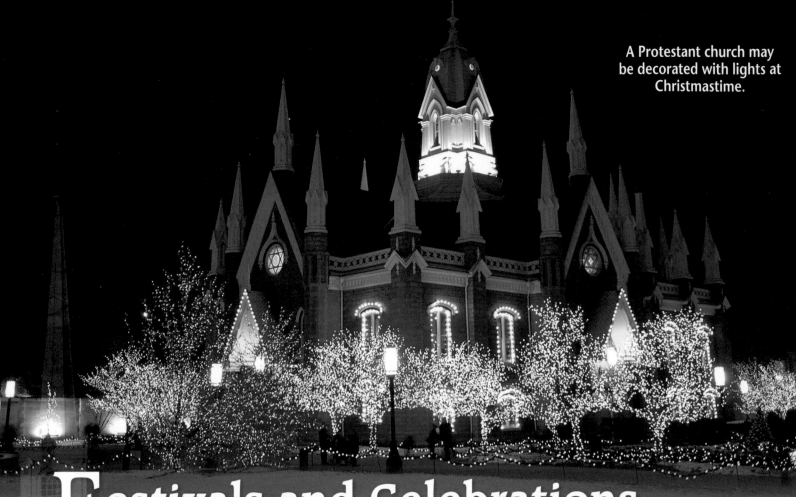

A Protestant church may be decorated with lights at Christmastime.

Festivals and Celebrations

Important celebrations for Protestants are Christmas, Palm Sunday, and Easter.

Hark! the herald angels sing,
"Glory to the newborn King!
Peace on Earth and mercy mild,
God and sinners reconciled!"
Joyful, all ye nations rise,
Join the triumph of the skies;
With the angelic host proclaim,
"Christ is born in Bethlehem."
Hark! the herald angels sing,
"Glory to the newborn King!"

"HARK THE HERALD ANGELS SING"
CHARLES WESLEY, 1743

Christmas

Christmas is celebrated on the 25th of December to celebrate the birth of Jesus Christ. Some Protestant churches place a brightly lit and decorated Christmas tree at the front of the church. Presents are placed under the tree for the poor during Advent, a time to spiritually prepare for Christmas. The presents are distributed so the families have them on Christmas Day.

On Christmas Day, Protestants usually attend a church service in the morning. They listen to Bible readings about Jesus and sing Christmas carols, such as "Hark the Herald Angels Sing." The minister, priest, or pastor preaches a sermon and plates are passed around to collect money for the poor. Sometimes, children put on a play about Jesus's birth. This is called a Nativity Play.

After church, Protestants have lunch with their friends and families and exchange gifts and cards.

Palm Sunday

Palm Sunday is one of the most important days in Lent, which is a time to prepare spiritually for Easter.

Palm Sunday is celebrated the Sunday before Easter. Christians remember that a group of people went to meet Jesus as he entered Jerusalem on a donkey. They waved palm branches and shouted his praises because they believed Jesus was the Messiah.

On Palm Sunday, some Protestant churches are decorated with palm branches. They may also give out a small piece of palm leaf made into the shape of a cross for people to pin to their clothes.

Worshippers follow the footsteps of Jesus during the traditional Palm Sunday procession into Jerusalem.

Easter

There are two days that are particularly important to Christians during Easter. They are Good Friday and Easter Sunday.

Good Friday is the day when Christians remember Jesus's **crucifixion**. Some Protestant churches drape the cross in the church in black.

Easter Sunday is the day when Christians remember Jesus's resurrection. Protestant churches are often decorated with bright flowers. In Western countries, Christians eat hot-cross buns and Easter eggs as part of their celebrations.

There are many holy days and festivals in the Protestant calendar. Here are some of them:

Lent
For the forty days before Easter
February, March, or April

Palm Sunday
March or April

Easter Sunday
March or April

Reformation Sunday
Lutherans commemorate Martin Luther challenging the teachings of the Catholic Church
Last Sunday in October

Advent
For the four weeks before Christmas
November and December

Christmas Day
December 25

Hot-cross buns are a popular food during Lent and Easter.

Important Protestants

Four important Protestants who brought about change in the Protestant Church were John and Charles Wesley and William and Catherine Booth.

John Wesley traveled to the United States as a missionary.

John and Charles Wesley
1703–1791 CE and 1707–1788 CE

Brothers John and Charles Wesley were originally Anglicans. They wanted a simpler church service with lots of hymns. They also felt the Anglican Church was neglecting the poor. The Wesleys and their followers began the Methodist movement. John administered the church and Charles preached and wrote over 7,000 hymns, many of which are still sung today. They also traveled around England taking care of, and preaching to, the poor.

Today there are Methodist churches in many parts of the world, particularly the United States, England, and some Pacific islands. In Australia, the Methodist Church became part of the Uniting Church in 1977.

O for a thousand tongues to sing my great Redeemer's praise, the glories of my God and King, the triumphs of his grace!

CHARLES WESLEY, 1739

Charles Wesley preached all over England.

William and Catherine Booth
1829–1912 CE and 1829–1890 CE

Husband and wife William and Catherine Booth began the Salvation Army in 1865 in London. They were originally Methodists, but wanted to spend time preaching to the poor, including alcoholics and people who could not cope and had dropped out of society.

William became famous for his preaching about forgiveness, his practical help and advice, and his beliefs about music. He was known for saying, "Why should the devil have all the best tunes?" The Salvation Army services have brass bands, people playing tambourines, and enthusiastic singing.

Catherine was famous for her preaching, fundraising, and counseling, her work with children and young people, and her campaigning against unfair laws, particularly against women. Catherine and William raised eight children, who all chose to work for the Salvation Army.

The Salvation Army is run like an army, with leaders called officers who wear a uniform. Members are called soldiers and most of them wear uniforms, too. The place in which they worship is called a Citadel.

Catherine Booth.
("The Mother of the Salvation Army")
1889.

Catherine and William Booth

Clothes and Food

Only members of the clergy must wear particular clothing in a Protestant church.

A Salvation Army officer in uniform

Protestants generally do not have to follow set rules on clothes, unless they are clergy. They also do not have many rules about food or drink.

Clothes for the Clergy

The Protestant church has a variety of traditions about what clothes members of the clergy should wear. Some, such as Anglican priests, wear a white robe, called an alb, and a stole, which is a long thin scarf. Others, such as pastors from the Assemblies of God Church, wear ordinary clothes to show that all Christian believers are equal. Salvation Army officers wear their uniform.

Clothes for Lay People

There are no rules about what Protestant lay people should wear to church. Many Protestants like to wear their best clothes to church.

Food

The Seventh-day Adventists are vegetarians. They also do not drink alcohol or smoke, and they encourage everyone to eat healthy food. The Sanitarium Health Food Company in Australia was set up by the Australian Seventh-day Adventist Church. In America, the Seventh-day Adventists run natural food stores and vegetarian restaurants. Seventh-day Adventists believe that eating or drinking should glorify God and preserve the health of the body, mind, and spirit.

Alcohol

Some denominations, including some Anglican churches, use wine for Holy Communion. Others, such as the Methodist Church and the Baptist Church, use grape juice instead. Some Protestants do not drink wine at all, such as members of the Salvation Army, Methodists, and some Baptists. They believe alcohol can cause bad behavior and health problems. There are also Bible verses that give warnings about drinking alcohol.

Some Protestant churches use grape juice instead of wine for Holy Communion.

Woe to those who rise early in the morning, that they may run after strong drink, who tarry late into the evening til wine inflames them.

Isaiah 5:11

And do not get drunk with wine, for that is debauchery.

Ephesians 5:18

21

The priest sprinkles holy water on the baby's head during a baptism.

Birth

When a baby is born into a Protestant family, the baby may be welcomed into the community by being baptized. Some Protestants do not believe in baptizing babies. They may choose to have a dedication ceremony instead.

Baptism

Baptism is the welcoming of a baby into the Protestant community. The ceremony is usually held at the church or in a home, hall, or garden. During the baptism service:

✝ the parents promise to raise the child to be a Christian

✝ the **godparents** promise to help the child to be a Christian if the parents are unable to

✝ the minister or priest sprinkles water on the baby's head

✝ the minister or priest **anoints** the baby's head with oil

✝ prayers are said to thank God for the baby.

Dedication Ceremony

Some Protestant churches, such as the Baptist Church, Church of Christ, and Assemblies of God Church, do not believe in infant baptism. They believe when people are old enough they can decide for themselves if they want to be baptized.

Parents can have a dedication ceremony instead of a baptism to welcome their baby to the church. This may be a private ceremony or part of a church service. The ceremony is similar to baptism but there is no anointing the baby with oil or sprinkling water on the baby. The parents make similar promises to the ones made in baptism and there are prayers to thank God for the baby.

After a baptism or dedication ceremony, there is sometimes a small party at the parents' home or the church hall, and the family is given gifts for the baby.

Some Protestants prefer to have a dedication ceremony for their baby instead of a baptism.

Girls from the town of Kirnbach in Germany dress in colorful local costumes for the confirmation ceremony.

Growing Up

An important ceremony for young Protestants growing up in some churches is confirmation. Other churches perform a believer's baptism ceremony.

Confirmation

Teenagers interested in the workings of their church and who wish to be committed to the church may ask the clergy if they can be confirmed. Confirmation makes them an adult member of the church.

Teenagers are encouraged to attend preparation classes to learn more about Christianity and to think about what their **faith** means to them. A Protestant confirmation must take place in a church. It is usually part of a church service and is a very simple ceremony. The teenagers confirm the promises that their parents made for them at their baptism.

Teenagers may receive a gift from the church, such as a certificate, to remember the day.

Adults who are **converts** to the faith may also choose to be confirmed as a sign of commitment to the church.

An adult baptism is a happy occasion.

Believer's Baptism

Some Protestant denominations, such as the Church of Christ, Baptists, Seventh-day Adventists, and the Assemblies of God, will only baptize people who have chosen to be baptized. They feel it is essential for the person being baptized to have made the decision themselves.

The believer's baptism may be held in a baptistery or in a special ceremony at a beach, river, lake, or swimming pool.

The person being baptized is briefly pushed underwater. This symbolizes the washing away of **sins** and the coming out of the water clean, rising to his or her new life as Christians. The person who conducts the baptism is usually a minister or pastor, who says, "I baptize you in the name of the Holy Trinity."

Adults who convert can have a baptism and a confirmation at the same service.

Marriage

The bride usually wears a white dress to the wedding to symbolize innocence and purity.

A Protestant wedding is a holy and legally binding occasion.

Beliefs About Marriage

Protestants have many strong beliefs about marriage. They believe that marriage:

✝ symbolizes the relationship between Jesus and the Church

✝ should last for life

✝ will teach couples more about God's love

✝ was created by God

✝ is a gift to be cherished and protected.

Protestants also believe that a person should not have sex before marriage, and they should only have sex with the person to whom they are married.

Beliefs About Divorce

Protestants believe that divorce is not what God wants and should not be encouraged. However, they do accept that people make mistakes. Most Protestant ministers will allow divorced people to remarry in their church.

Wedding Ceremony

A Protestant wedding ceremony is legally binding. It is often held in the church, although some weddings are held in parks or gardens, or even on the beach.

During the ceremony, the couple promise that they will always love, respect, and be faithful to each other, in good and bad times. The clergy delivers a sermon about marriage and there are hymns, prayers, and often Bible readings by family and friends. The couple exchange rings to symbolize the unbroken bonds of marriage and the clergy introduces the couple to the congregation as husband and wife.

After the ceremony, the couple sign the wedding certificate.

27

Death and the Afterlife

Protestants have important customs that they practice after a person dies. They also believe in an afterlife.

The Funeral

When Protestants die, family and friends organize a funeral service for them. The funeral is usually held within a week of the person dying. The body is placed in a coffin and the lid may be open or closed for the funeral service, depending on what the family prefers.

Protestants may choose to bury or **cremate** their dead. They believe that the soul goes to Heaven without the body. The funeral service can be held at the church, at a crematorium, or in a park. If the body is being cremated, there may be services at the church and crematorium.

Funerals are a time for family and friends to say goodbye to their loved ones. Clergy and other believers reassure mourners that the person is not lost to them but living in Heaven with God, Jesus, and the Holy Spirit. The service may include the person's favorite hymns, **eulogies**, and special prayers.

The service ends when the coffin is carried from the church and taken to the cemetery for burial or the crematorium for cremation.

After the church service, the coffin is carried to the cemetery for burial.

Life After Death

Protestants believe that when they die, their soul will go to heaven to be with God. They believe that Jesus' death took the punishment for their sins. God is perfect so he cannot live in the presence of sin. Someone had to bear the punishment for people's sins, so Jesus took these sins with him when he died on the cross.

Protestants believe no matter how many times they let God down on Earth, they will spend eternity with the Holy Trinity. This does not mean they can do evil actions on Earth and get away with it when they die. They must always pray for forgiveness for their sins and avoid sinning, with the Holy Spirit's help.

Heaven and Hell

Protestants believe in heaven and hell. The Bible describes heaven as:

† a beautiful, peaceful place where there is no crying or fighting

† a place where there is room for anyone who has expressed faith in Jesus

† a place where people become like angels

† a place where there are many good things that will never fade or rot.

Hell is a place where people are separated from God forever. Protestants who interpret the Bible literally believe that people who do not believe in Jesus will go to hell.

The cross, seen on many Protestant gravestones, symbolizes Jesus taking the punishment for people's sins when he was crucified.

Protestantism Around the World

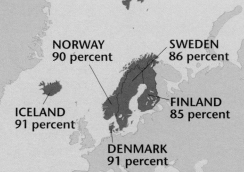

Christianity is the world's biggest religion. There are approximately 2 billion Christians in the world. Around 593 million of them are Protestants. Protestants are found in most parts of the world, such as the United States, Britain, Australia, New Zealand, Africa, and Europe.

There are about 90 million Baptists, 77 million Anglicans, 70 million Lutherans, 50 million members of the Assemblies of God Church, 16 million Seventh-day Adventists, 11 million Methodists, 2 million members of the Church of Christ, and 350,000 Quakers throughout the world. Salvation Army membership includes more than 5 million officers, soldiers, and volunteers.

This map shows the top ten Protestant countries.

ARCTIC OCEAN

ARCTIC OCEAN

NORWAY
90 percent

SWEDEN
86 percent

ICELAND
91 percent

FINLAND
85 percent

DENMARK
91 percent

BAHAMAS
76 percent

ATLANTIC
OCEAN

PACIFIC
OCEAN

PACIFIC
OCEAN

St. KITTS AND NEVIS
83 percent

ANTIGUA AND BARBUDA
86 percent

TUVALU
98 percent

St. VINCENT AND THE GRENADINES
77 percent

INDIAN OCEAN

N
W—E
S

KEY

▬	area of country
BARBADOS	name of country
67 percent	percentage of country population that is Protestant

SOUTHERN OCEAN

SOUTHERN OCEAN

Glossary

anoints	when a member of the clergy pours holy oil or water on someone's forehead
apartheid	the former policy in South Africa of separating groups based on their race
apostles	those who saw Jesus Christ after he rose from the dead and told people about it, and also Paul, who heard, rather than saw, Jesus
baptistery	a small pool in a church, wide enough for two people, that is used for believer's baptisms
clergy	ordained members of the church, such as priests or pastors
congregation	the people attending a church service
converts	people who come to believe in a religion later in life
cremate	to burn a dead body until only ashes are left
crucifixion	death by being nailed to a wooden cross
denomination	a branch of Christianity, such as Catholic or Protestant
disciples	followers of Jesus
eulogies	speeches about a dead person's life
faith	belief in the teachings of religion
godparents	adults who are not the child's parents but who promise to guide the child in the Christian faith
Holy Trinity	the Father, the Son, and the Holy Spirit
lay people	members of the church who are not members of the clergy
Messiah	in Christianity, the savior of all Christians, Jesus Christ
prophets	people through whom the will of God is expressed
Purgatory	the place where, according to Catholicism, souls are cleansed and prepared for life in heaven
resurrection	to come back to life
scriptures	sacred writings
sermon	a speech explaining a verse of the Bible and advice on how people can use it in their daily lives
sins	bad actions, wrongs
souls	people's spirits, which live forever

Index

A

Advent,   17
Anglican Church,   5, 7, 9, 18, 20, 21, 30
Archbishop Desmond Tutu,   9
Assemblies of God Church,   5, 20, 23, 25, 30

B

baptism,   22, 23, 24, 25
Baptist Church,   5, 21, 23, 25, 30
Bible,   10–11, 12, 13, 14, 21, 27, 29
burial,   28

C

Catherine Booth,   18, 19
Catholic Church,   5, 12, 13
Charles Wesley,   18
Christmas,   16
Church of Christ,   5, 23, 25, 30
clergy,   7, 14, 15, 20, 24, 27, 28
clothing,   20
confirmation,   24, 25
cremation,   28
crucifixion,   17, 29

D

dedication ceremony,   23
divorce,   26

E

Easter,   16, 17

F

forgiveness,   9, 12, 19, 29
funerals,   28

G

godparents,   22
Good Friday,   17
Gospels (Matthew, Mark, Luke, and John),   10, 11
grape juice,   15, 21

H

heaven,   5, 6, 12, 28, 29
hell,   29
Holy Communion,   7, 14, 15, 21
holy days,   14, 16–17
Holy Trinity,   6, 25, 29
hymns,   14, 18, 27, 28

J

John Wesley,   18

L

Lent,   17
Lord's Prayer,   6
Lutheran Church,   5, 12, 30

M

Martin Luther,   12
Messiah,   6, 11, 17
Methodist Church,   5, 18, 19, 21, 30
missionaries,   8
music,   19

N

New Testament,   10, 11, 12, 13

O

Old Testament,   10, 11
Orthodox Church,   5

P

Palm Sunday,   16, 17
prayers,   6, 12, 14, 15, 22, 23, 27, 28
Protestant Church floor plan,   14
Proverbs,   10
Psalms,   10
purgatory,   12

Q

Quakers (Religious Society of Friends),   5, 15, 30

R

resurrection,   5, 17

S

Salvation Army,   5, 8, 15, 19, 20, 21, 30
Sanitarium Health Food Company,   21
Sermon on the Mount,   9
Seventh-day Adventist Church,   5, 21, 25, 30

U

Uniting Church,   18

W

weddings,   26–7
William Booth,   18, 19
William Tyndale,   12, 13
wine,   15, 21
world distribution of Protestants,   30